ILLUSION ART

Jane Bingham

Heinemann Library
Chicago, Illinois

Produced for Heinemann Library by
White-Thomson Publishing Ltd.
Designed by Tim Mayer
Printed and bound in China by South China Printing Company.

11 10 09 08 07
10 9 8 7 6 5 4 3 2 1

Library of Congress Cataloging-in-Publication Data
Bingham, Jane.
 Illusion art / Jane Bingham.
   p. cm. -- (Art off the wall)
 Includes index.
 ISBN-10: 1-4034-8290-X (library binding-hardcover)
 1. Optical illusions in art--Juvenile literature. I. Title. II. Series.
 N7430.5.B53 2006
 701'.8--dc22

                    2006005740

Acknowledgments
The publisher would like to thank the following for their kind permission to use their photographs:
akg-images/Tri Star Pictures/Album p. **21**; Bridgeman Art Library pp. 8 (Collection of the Earl of Leicester, Holkham Hall), **12**, **22–23** (© Rafael Valls Gallery, London), **32** (National Gallery, London), **47** (National Gallery, London); Corbis pp. **10–11** (Louis K. Meisel Gallery, Inc.), **15** (Bettmann), **14** (Images.com), **25** (Charles Bell), **44–45** (Christie's Images), **48–49** (Pitchal Frederic); © 2005 The M.C. Escher Company, Holland, front cover, p. **17**; Patrick Hughes p. **18**; Mary Evans Picture Library p. **39**; Syd Mead pp. **26–27**; István Orosz pp. **33**, **34–35**; John Pugh p. **4**, **28–29**; Patrick Snels p. **40**; Topfoto p. **13** (J Almasi/UPPA/Photoshot), **36** (Noa/Rober-Viollet); Anthony Waichulis pp. **5**, **24**; Design/Photography (c) Kurt Wenner 2006 pp. **6**, **31**.

The artwork on pages 7, 9, 11, 16, 19, 20, 37, 38, 41, 42, 43, 45, and 46 was created by Peter Bull Art Studio.

Cover photograph: M.C. Escher, *Waterfall*, © The M.C. Escher Company, Holland

Every effort has been made to contact copyright holders of any material reproduced in this book. Any omissions will be rectified in subsequent printings if notice is given to the publishers.

Contents

What Is Illusion Art? 4

Depth and Distance 6

Playing Tricks 16

Super-Realism 22

Different Viewpoints 30

Puzzling Patterns 40

Optical Investigations 44

Taking It Further 48

Glossary 52

Find Out More 54

Index 56

Words appearing in the text in bold, **like this**, are explained in the Glossary.

what Is Illusion Art?

You are walking down a city street, when suddenly you notice something strange. One of the buildings has a gaping hole in its side. You look again and see an amazing sight. Inside the building is a Mexican temple!

Behind the broken wall is a flight of steps flanked by carved lions. A girl is just about to step inside the temple. You race across the street to join her, but realize just in time that you are heading straight for a solid wall!

What on earth is happening here?

The broken wall, the temple, and the girl are all part of an **optical illusion**. The whole scene is a **mural**. By using a range of skills and techniques, the artist has managed to create the illusion that his painted scene is solid and "real."

This mural in Los Gatos, California, was painted by the U.S. illusion artist John Pugh. Pugh created the mural after a major earthquake shook the town in 1989. Its title, *Siete Punto Uno* ("Seven Point One"), refers to the strength of the earthquake. You can find out more about Pugh's work on pages 28–29.

Many illusion artists play tricks with the viewer. Looking at this painting, *Foul Ball!*, by U.S. artist Anthony Waichulis, it is hard to decide exactly what you are seeing. Are you looking at a picture with a broken glass frame, or are you seeing a baseball through a broken window?

Illusion art forms

Illusion art can take several different forms. Many illusion artists use their skills to make you believe that their flat, two-dimensional (**2D**) paintings are three-dimensional (**3D**) and really have depth. Others create impossible structures that confuse your brain, making you think that what you see makes sense, even though you know it cannot really exist. Some illusion art plays tricks with your eyes, so that one moment you see something and the next you do not. Some illusion artists can even make you see shapes and colors that are not really there at all.

Skills and techniques

Creating illusions is not easy. Illusion artists have to practice for years to learn the skills they need. This book explores the techniques and tricks used by illusion artists and gives some useful tips on how to create your own illusions. In the final chapter there are suggestions for a range of careers using 3D drawing and modeling skills.

Try it yourself

Throughout this book are suggestions for illusions that you can try yourself. For most of these activities, you will need a sketchpad, a pencil, a ruler, and an eraser.

None of the activities described in this book involves the use of a computer. However, you will find some suggestions for computer-based activities in the websites listed at the back of the book.

Depth and Distance

How do artists create the illusion that an object painted on a flat surface is solid and real? How do they make a room have depth, so that it looks as though you could step inside it? And how do they show scenes that seem to stretch into the distance? The answer is that they follow the rules of **perspective**.

In addition to using perspective, artists rely on some other methods to create the illusion of depth and distance. The use of **shading** can make people and objects seem more solid and real. Gradually fading the colors in the background of a painting gives a sense of distance.

The technique of **foreshortening** (showing things larger when they are really close up) helps to create an illusion of depth. All of these techniques will be discussed in this chapter.

Using perspective

Whenever artists want to create the illusion of a 3D image on a flat surface, they use the rules of perspective. Whether they are showing figures in a room, a city scene, or a car speeding into the distance, they still follow the same basic rules. Once you have learned how to use the rules of perspective, you can create 3D images of your own.

In his painting *The Magic Flute*, the U.S. artist Kurt Wenner uses a range of methods to achieve the illusion of depth and distance. The painting follows the rules of perspective. Some figures in the **foreground** are foreshortened, and the colors gradually fade into the distance. You can find out more about Wenner's work on page 30.

How perspective works

Everybody knows that things seem to get smaller as they get farther away. You can see this clearly when you look at a railroad track. As the track disappears into the distance, the two lines seem to get closer. Eventually the two lines seem to meet at a distant point on the **horizon line**. In art, this point is called the **vanishing point**.

When artists use perspective, they use the horizon line and the vanishing point as the starting points for their picture. Then, they create a set of **construction lines**, which all lead to the vanishing point. These lines help the artist show objects from exactly the right angle, and this makes the objects appear solid and real.

Discovering perspective

One of the first artists to use perspective was the Italian Philippo Brunelleschi, who lived in the 15th century. Brunelleschi realized that buildings look smaller as they get farther away. He painted some buildings in the city of Florence using perspective. Then, he showed his paintings to other artists and asked them to compare them to the real buildings. Very soon, artists all over Italy were using perspective.

This simple picture has been created using a horizon line, a vanishing point, and construction lines.

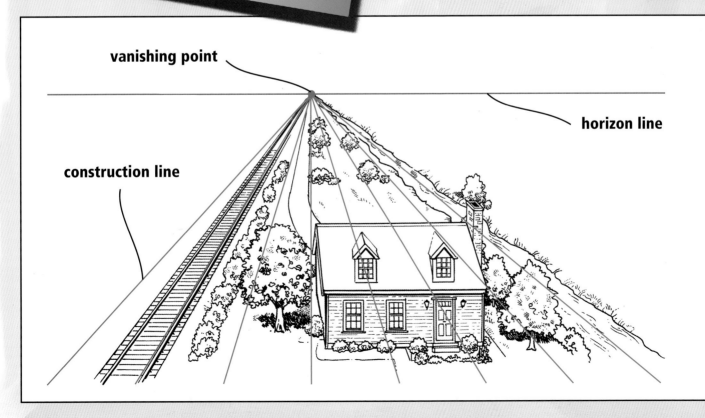

vanishing point

horizon line

construction line

Shadows and shading

Even if buildings and objects are drawn in perfect perspective, they will not look solid and real unless they have shadows and shading. Whether you are copying a scene from an existing picture or drawing from imagination, think about where the light is coming from and where the shadows fall. Then, shade the sides of the object that do not get any light. Remember, shadows fall in exactly the opposite direction from the source of the light.

A distant haze

About 100 years after perspective was discovered, some artists noticed an interesting visual effect. When they looked into the distance, features of the landscape such as trees and hills seemed to become paler. They decided to try out ways to show this effect.

Atmospheric perspective

A group of artists in Italy began to experiment with a new technique. They painted the hills that were in the distance a grayish blue and gradually blended one color into another to create a hazy effect. This technique was called *sfumato*, which comes from the Italian word for "smoke." Ever since then, artists have used smoky blues and grays to create convincing distant scenes. Today, the *sfumato* technique is known as **atmospheric perspective**.

This is called *A Sunset* or *Landscape with Argus Guarding Io*, and it was painted in the 17th century by the French artist Claude Lorraine. He was a master of atmospheric perspective. Notice how the strong colors and shapes in the foreground gradually fade into hazy blue in the distance.

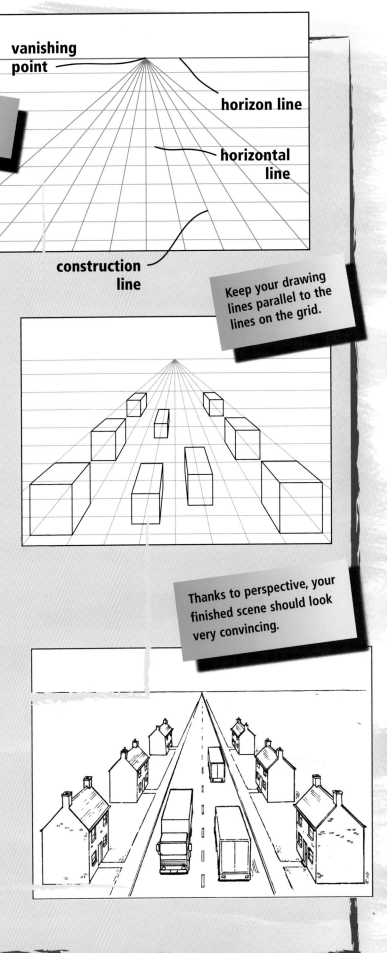

vanishing point

horizon line

horizontal line

construction line

Mark your construction lines lightly in pencil.

Keep your drawing lines parallel to the lines on the grid.

Thanks to perspective, your finished scene should look very convincing.

Why not try creating a simple 3D street scene, following the rules of perspective?

1 Use a ruler and pencil to draw a horizon line close to the top of the page.

2 Mark the vanishing point in the center of the horizon line.

3 Draw a central construction line from the vanishing point to the bottom of the page.

4 Keeping the top of your ruler on the vanishing point, move the base of your ruler outward to the right, step-by-step, marking construction lines as you go. Do this about five times, making sure that the top of the ruler is always on the vanishing point.

5 Return your ruler to the central construction line and move it to the left, step-by-step, marking construction lines. Do this about five times.

6 Now, draw a series of **horizontal** lines below the horizon line. These horizontal lines will cross the construction lines to give you a helpful drawing **grid**.

7 Using your grid lines as a guide, draw some rectangles. Some can be buildings and some can be trucks.

8 When you have finished your drawing, outline your objects in ink. Then, rub out your pencil guidelines.

9 Now, add shading and shadows to make your buildings look solid. If you are using color, make the buildings in the distance a slightly lighter shade.

What's your point of view?

When artists use a single vanishing point to create a scene, they are using **one-point perspective**. This simple form of perspective can be very effective in creating the illusion that something has depth. But one-point perspective does have a very serious drawback. In order to make the illusion work, everything in the picture has to be viewed straight on.

Looking from the side

If artists want to show the side of an object as well as its front, they need to use two vanishing points. Perspective using two vanishing points is known as **two-point perspective**. Artists use two-point perspective to show buildings and objects that are seen partly from the side.

Try it yourself

Why not try using two-point perspective to draw a simple building?

1 Use your ruler and pencil to draw a horizon line close to the top of a piece of paper. Mark two vanishing points on the horizon, as far apart as possible.

2 Draw a short **vertical** line in the center of the picture, below the horizon line. This will be the front corner line of your building. Then, draw construction lines from the top and bottom of this line to each vanishing point (the red lines).

3 Next, draw a vertical line to the left of your front corner line, between the top and bottom construction lines. From the top and bottom of this line, draw construction lines to the right vanishing point (the blue lines).

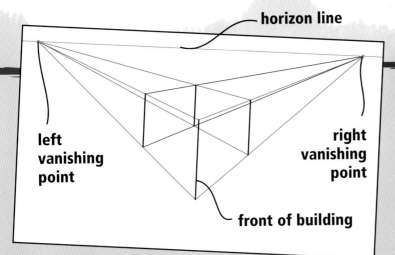

In this street scene, *Tony's*, U.S artist Anthony Brunelli used two-point perspective to create the illusion that his scene has depth.

Three views at once

Sometimes artists need to show three sides of an object. For example, an artist may want to show a building from the side and the front and also from the top. To show this point of view, you need to have three vanishing points and use three-point perspective. Artists use three-point perspective to create impressive visual effects, such as the view from the top of a skyscraper.

horizon line

left vanishing point

right vanishing point

front of building

First, create a drawing grid like this.

Add details and shading to create your finished picture.

4 Draw a similar vertical line to the right of your front corner line. From the top and bottom of this line, draw construction lines to the left vanishing point (the green lines).

5 At the point where the top construction lines meet, draw a vertical line to the meeting point of the bottom construction lines. This is the back corner of your building.

6 Now, rub out the construction lines and any lines inside the building. Add some windows, a door, and a roof.

"Real" rooms

The rules of perspective can be used in outdoor and indoor scenes. Artists use perspective to help them create convincing **interiors**. In the 17th century, a group of Dutch painters began to show the insides of houses in a very realistic way. Artists such as Jan Vermeer and Pieter de Hooch painted people in the rooms of their houses. These simple rooms, with their black-and-white tiled floors, were the perfect subject to show off the painters' skill in using the rules of perspective.

Perspective boxes

Some Dutch artists became so interested in showing realistic rooms that they created **perspective boxes**. These were 3D models of interiors created from wooden boxes. Inside the boxes, the tops, bottoms, and sides were painted using the rules of perspective, so they appeared to be real 3D rooms. The viewer looked through a hole on the side of the box to see the room, which looked amazingly solid and real.

In his 17th-century painting *A Family in an Interior*, Hendrik van der Burgh has used perspective to make a room look solid and real. He even manages to show a glimpse of another room beyond.

Stage sets

Stage set designers often need to create the illusion of a room or another space, such as a garden. One of the ways they do this is by using tall, painted boards that are placed at an angle on either side of the stage. These boards, known as **flats**, are painted using the rules of perspective to give the impression of walls, pillars, or arches stretching backward. Meanwhile, the scene at the rear of the stage (known as the **backdrop**) is painted using atmospheric perspective to give a sense of distance.

Toy theaters

In the 19th century, artists began to make miniature theaters for children. The most famous creator of toy theaters was Benjamin Pollock. Pollock's toy theaters create a convincing sense of 3D space through their use of flats and backdrops.

A magic room

In 2005 the British artist Stuart Pearson Wright created a very unusual portrait of J. K. Rowling. He showed the author of *Harry Potter* writing at a table inside a 3D room. In order to create his magical illusion, Wright placed a cut-out portrait of the writer inside a shallow box, which was painted in perspective to make it look like a room. Wright says his portrait was inspired by the art of toy theaters.

Stuart Pearson Wright's *Portrait of J. K. Rowling* invites the viewer to stare and wonder. Wright creates the illusion that Rowling is sitting inside a small, bare room. The author is deliberately shown too big for the room, as if she is trapped inside a magical space.

Foreshortening

When artists want to create the illusion that a scene or an object has depth, they follow the rules of perspective. Sometimes they also use a technique called foreshortening. Artists use foreshortening in the foreground of a picture when they want to show objects or figures that are coming straight toward the viewer. For example, the figure of a man who is pointing at the viewer would be shown with his finger, hand, and arm foreshortened.

What is foreshortening?

When artists use the technique of foreshortening, they are recreating the visual effect that you experience when you see an object or figure coming straight toward you. When someone points straight at you, you cannot see the full length of his or her arm. It appears to be shorter.

As something comes toward you, it seems to get bigger, just as things in the distance appear smaller. You can see this effect for yourself by standing in front of a full-length mirror with both fists clenched. Raise one arm toward the mirror and keep your other arm by your side. Notice the size of the fist that is coming toward you, compared with the fist by your side, and see how short your raised arm looks compared with your other arm.

In this comic strip image, the artist has used foreshortening to create a dramatic effect. It makes you feel that the hero is flying straight toward you!

Comic foreshortening

Comic strip artists use an exaggerated form of foreshortening. A standard comic image is the angry man heading straight toward you with his fist raised. The foreshortened fist is shown so large that it takes up most of the picture!

This painted scene shows God creating the Sun, Moon, and planets. It comes from the ceiling of the Sistine Chapel in Rome, painted by the artist Michelangelo between 1508 and 1512. Michelangelo's striking figure of God the Creator, with his large pointing finger and greatly shortened arm, is a famous early example of foreshortening.

Try it yourself

Ceiling art

Some of the most spectacular examples of foreshortening can be seen on ceilings. In some ceiling paintings, the painted figures seem to lean right out of the picture toward you.

One of the early masters of ceiling painting was the Italian artist Michelangelo, who lived in the 16th century. His paintings for the ceiling of the Sistine Chapel in Rome include some dramatically foreshortened figures.

You can practice foreshortening by getting a friend to pose for you. Sit on the floor at the end of a bed and ask your friend to lie on the bed with his or her feet toward you. Then, draw what you see. You can also reverse the pose so your friend's head is nearest to you. The trick is to believe your eyes and draw exactly what you see!

Playing Tricks

Some artists play tricks with perspective in order to create their optical illusions. These artists know how to follow the rules of perspective to create the illusion of depth. However, they deliberately confuse us by creating "impossible objects" in their art. These impossible objects cannot really exist, even though they seem to obey the rules of perspective.

Escher's impossible buildings

The 20th-century Belgian artist M. C. Escher was a master of trick perspective. He depicted many "impossible buildings" that fool the viewer's senses. At first sight, these buildings appear to make sense as solid structures. However, when you look carefully, you realize that they could not possibly stand up.

Escher's buildings contain staircases that lead nowhere, arches that rest in space, and water channels that flow upward. One of his most famous works is *Waterfall* (shown opposite). It shows a water system in which the water is constantly—and impossibly—recycled. In another of his works, *Concave and Convex*, floors become ceilings and a building appears to be seen sometimes from the outside and sometimes from the inside.

Drawing "impossible buildings" like this requires careful planning. Escher thought about the structures in *Concave and Convex* for over a month before he decided how to show them.

What's the secret?

One of Escher's techniques was to move the vanishing points around in his paintings. This allowed him to show part of a building from above and another part from below. Both of the viewpoints are perfectly shown, so that they both seem correct to the viewer, but Escher's trick was to combine two or more viewpoints in one picture. Escher also used shading very skillfully to trick you into believing that the impossible objects you see are really solid.

Try it yourself

Copy the impossible staircase shown here, and then use your drawing to confuse your friends!

One of Escher's favorite structures was the "endless staircase" that seemed to keep going down forever. He used it in many of his drawings and it has been copied many times, both as a drawing and as a model. See if you can draw an endless staircase. Why do you think it tricks the viewer?

Escher's drawing *Waterfall* is filled with puzzles and mysteries. The water tower is so skillfully drawn that the viewer is almost persuaded that the water in the channels can flow uphill!

Gonsalves's puzzles

The contemporary Canadian artist Rob Gonsalves creates playful **fantasy** images that play tricks with perspective. *Treehouse in Autumn* shows a house that is half on the ground and half in a tree. *On the Upswing* presents a dizzying landscape seen from several different viewpoints.

Another of Gonsalves's paintings, *Castle on the Cliff,* plays fascinating games with the idea of size. The children in this painting are busy making a castle. However, it is impossible for the viewer to decide whether the castle is normal size and the children are giants, or whether the castle is smaller and the children are normal size. (You can find details of a website containing images of Gonsalves's work on page 54.)

Hughes's reverspectives

In the 1960s the British artist Patrick Hughes began to paint on canvases arranged as a series of pyramids sticking out of the wall toward the viewer. He called these paintings "reverspectives."

Hughes's reverspectives are designed to be seen by viewers on the move. As the viewers walk along the length of the painting, they see the picture from slightly different angles. This changing viewpoint creates disturbing optical illusions, as the painted shapes and objects in the picture appear to move in front of the viewers' eyes!

Patrick Hughes's work *Sharperspective* presents a dramatic image, even when shown like this on a flat page. However, you need to see his reverspectives in 3D in order to experience their constantly shifting shapes.

Can you believe your eyes?

Take a careful look at the picture of two monsters in a tunnel. What exactly do you see? Most people would say a big monster chasing a small one. But this is wrong. In fact, the two monsters are exactly the same size!

This simple optical illusion shows how easy it is to confuse the viewer by playing tricks with perspective. The tunnel in the picture follows the rules of perspective and is much smaller at the far end than it is at the front. So, when you look at the picture, you expect the figure at the end of the tunnel to follow the rules of perspective, too, and get smaller.

However, when drawing the figures, the artist has ignored the rules of perspective and drawn both monsters exactly the same size. The one at the back seems bigger than the one in front because your brain expects it to be very small.

Look at these two monsters in a tunnel and compare their sizes. Can you really trust your eyes?

Changing shapes

Some shapes seem to change in front of our eyes, as our brains try to make sense of them. One example of this is the cube shown here.

Where is the blue face of this cube? Is it at the front or the back? Now, keep on looking—where is the blue face now? As you look at the cube, it appears to flip so that the blue face is sometimes at the back and sometimes at the front.

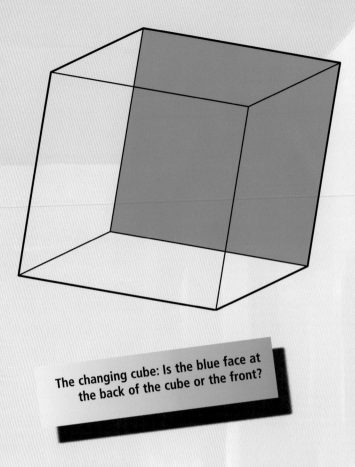

The changing cube: Is the blue face at the back of the cube or the front?

What is happening?

When you look at the 2D drawing of the cube, your brain automatically creates a 3D object. But the drawing does not give enough information for your brain to know exactly how the cube should look. Your brain makes a "best guess" about how the cube works. But then it tries another guess, so the blue face flips from the back to the front. M. C. Escher often used this effect in his impossible buildings, which appear to keep changing in front of your eyes.

Impossible images

Look carefully at this picture of a tricky trident. Does it have three prongs or two? Now, cover the ends of the prong. What do you see now? When you first look at it, the trident appears to have three prongs. But after a while you realize that this is impossible.

Impossible images like this trident demonstrate the fact that our brains automatically try to make sense of a shape, even when it cannot be done. When they create their impossible images, illusion artists are taking advantage of our instinct to make sense of what we see.

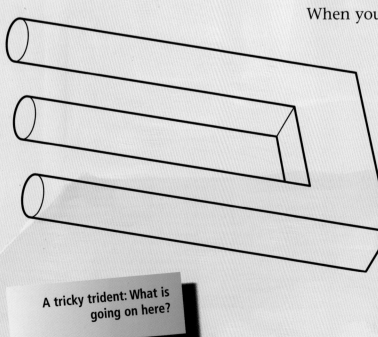

A tricky trident: What is going on here?

Scary effects

The "impossible buildings" made famous by Escher have been used in video games and movies to create nightmare castles and dungeons from which people can never escape. The movie *Labyrinth*, made in 1986 and starring David Bowie, includes a terrifying scene in which the heroine is trapped in a castle that is based on an Escher drawing.

In the movie *Labyrinth* David Bowie plays an evil goblin king who lives in an "impossible castle" that closely resembles the drawings of Escher. The teenage heroine, Sarah, has an Escher poster on her bedroom wall. But fantasy turns to reality when Sarah has to find her way through the goblin's castle to rescue her younger brother.

Super-Realism

Have you ever seen a painting that seemed so real you wanted to touch it, just to be sure that it was not the real thing? Today, this style of incredibly realistic art is known as **super-realism** or, sometimes, **photorealism**, because it looks almost like a photograph. But realistic art has a very long history. Over 2,000 years ago, artists were using their skill to create the illusion that the objects that they painted were actually real.

Trompe l'oeil paintings

The art of painting objects to look completely real began with the ancient Greeks more than 2,000 years ago. But the style really took off in the 15th century, when artists painted flowers and insects on the borders of prayer books. The flowers seemed to cast real shadows and the butterflies looked as though they had just landed on the page. This kind of art was given the name *trompe l'oeil* (pronounced "tromp loy"), which is French for "trick the eye."

Coin trick

In the 17th century, the great Dutch artist Rembrandt taught his students to paint in a very realistic style. In return, the students played a trick on their master. They painted coins on the floor of Rembrandt's studio, and then enjoyed watching him try to pick them up!

Early letter-rack paintings

By the 1600s artists were using *trompe l'oeil* techniques to create "letter-rack" paintings. These showed collections of letters, cards, and pictures that all seemed to be fixed to a board. When people first saw these letter-rack pictures, some of them tried to pluck the objects out of the paintings!

Later letter-rack painters

The art of letter-rack painting was taken up by a group of U.S. artists in the 19th century. Artists such as John Frederick Peto and William Harnett showed collections of objects attached to doors and bulletin boards. (Turn to page 54 to find details of websites containing images by the U.S. letter-rack painters.)

This early letter-rack painting was created by the Dutch artist Edwaert Colyer in 1703. The artist has deliberately shown off his skill by painting objects with a wide range of **textures**.

Modern trompe l'oeil

Some contemporary *trompe l'oeil* painters in the United States have adapted the letter-rack tradition to show objects from the modern world. The artist Molly Springfield creates paintings featuring collections of matchbooks and crumpled receipts. Artist Anthony Waichulis shows folded and torn dollar bills and opened envelopes containing letters and photos. Artist David Brega often shows objects inside cupboards. A popular subject for *trompe l'oeil* artists is a dartboard with a single dart sticking into it.

This is *Pieces of History* by Anthony Waichulis. This painting is more than just a very well-done *trompe l'oeil*. The carefully chosen objects also tell a story.

Super shadows

One reason why *trompe l'oeil* paintings work so well is because their artists pay special attention to the shadows cast by objects. Even a flat object like a (slightly crumpled) dollar bill casts a strong shadow on the surface underneath it.

Painting or photo?

During the 1960s, a new art movement known as photorealism began in the United States. Photorealist artists painted objects, people, and scenes in a style that looked very much like photography.

In the 1960s and 1970s, Richard Estes and Robert Cottingham specialized in street scenes with elaborate reflections in glass windows. Chuck Close produced portraits that looked like photos, and Charles Bell painted colorful toys and pinball machines. Meanwhile, Ralph Goings concentrated on diners.

Goings showed the interiors of the diners, but he also painted close-ups of tables featuring plates of food. (You can find details of websites with images of photorealist works on page 54.)

Photorealist techniques

Photorealist artists work from photographs, copying them again and again until they can reproduce their effects exactly in paint. These artists are especially interested in showing the ways that objects reflect light. They often choose to paint very shiny objects so that they can show the reflections on an object's surfaces.

50 Points When Lit is one of many paintings of pinball machines created by the artist Charles Bell. Like most photorealist artists, Bell was fascinated with colorful, shiny surfaces and reflections.

Realistic sculpture

Some artists have created amazing sculptures in the super-realist style. Until her death in 2005, Canadian sculptor Marilyn Levine made clay models of everyday objects, such as a pair of battered cowboy boots, an abandoned backpack, and a leather jacket hanging from a hook.

The U.S. artist Duane Hanson produced life-sized figures of ordinary people. Hanson's figures include a woman pushing a grocery cart, a salesman, a museum guard, and a janitor. When people come across Hanson's figures in art galleries, they often start to talk to them—until they realize they are not real!

Fantasy art

Many artists use super-realistic techniques and styles to create fantasy scenes for magazines, books, computer games, and movies. Fantasy artists choose vivid colors and glossy surfaces to create **futuristic** scenes set on other planets or enchanted worlds of castles and forests.

Super-realistic fantasy art is a popular style for computer games. Artists create hundreds of drawings—known as visuals—showing the characters and scenes that will be used in the games. Then, these visuals are turned into 3D **animations**. Fantasy artists need to be very skilled at drawing. Nothing breaks the spell of a fantasy faster than a character or a scene that does not look convincing!

Syd Mead: Fantasy artist

One of today's leading fantasy artists is Syd Mead, the creator of visuals for science fiction movies such as *Blade Runner*, *Aliens*, and *Mission to Mars*. In his paintings, Mead skillfully uses the techniques of perspective and foreshortening, combined with a sound understanding of **engineering**.

Syd Mead's *Running of the Six DRGXX* (1983) is a dramatic image of six racing robots. It was designed as a publicity poster for the Tokyo International Sport Fair. The poster displays Mead's skill at foreshortening, shading, and perspective—as well as his ability to create a very exciting scene.

Once he has drawn in all the underlying structures, Mead uses an **airbrush** to create a range of different surfaces. His scenes are usually shown in strong sunlight, with very dark shadows to emphasize the exciting shapes of his buildings and vehicles.

Airbrush effects

Airbrushes use compressed air to blow paint onto a surface. By adjusting the ink flow from the brush, artists can produce fine lines, soft tones, and solid areas of color. Artists also use an airbrush to merge different colors into each other and to fade a color to white. These techniques are especially useful for showing highlights and reflections on shiny surfaces.

Trompe l'oeil murals

The U.S. illusion artist John Pugh creates large-scale murals that work as giant *trompe l'oeil* paintings. Sometimes his murals show just architecture, but often they include people, plants, and animals within a striking architectural setting.

Like many *trompe l'oeil* paintings, Pugh's murals are often jokey and playful. The side of the college library in El Paso, California, is shown as a crumbling brick wall, which reveals a series of classical columns underneath. A mural in the Cherry Creek Shopping Center in Denver, Colorado, shows a young woman reaching up to pick cherries from a tree.

On the wall of a building in Winslow, Arizona, Pugh painted a 1950s shop front with *trompe l'oeil* windows. A downstairs window shows the reflection of a passing truck, driven by a woman who has slowed down to look at the illusion that she is part of! On an upstairs windowsill sits a bird, and through another window a couple can be seen embracing.

They look so real!

Pugh's murals are so realistic that they often cause confusion. Several people have tried to talk to his painted characters and walk into rooms that are not really there. But Pugh does not just use illusion as a game. His works are also intended to make people think.

Many of Pugh's murals comment on the purpose of a building or reflect the history of a place, and some of his works are quite disturbing. Pugh's *Roots* series shows *trompe l'oeil* roots and branches of trees breaking through brick walls, demonstrating the indestructible power of nature.

Making the murals

After he has studied the site for a mural, Pugh creates a series of sketches. Then, he uses these sketches to make an accurate drawing for his mural, known as a **cartoon**. Pugh creates a photographic slide from his cartoon, which he projects full-size onto the painting surface. He traces his design onto the wall, correcting any mistakes in drawing or perspective.

Pugh uses color-fast **acrylic** mural paint. He pays particular attention in his paintings to how light is reflected and how it casts shadows. Pugh says, "I couldn't create the illusions I do without understanding the workings of light."

In 1980, after studying art at North California State University, Pugh painted his first large-scale mural on the side of the college library. The mural, called *Academe*, is a witty comment on the ancient history of learning.

Different Viewpoints

Sometimes artists create an illusion that can only be seen from a certain point of view. If you approach these works of art from the right direction, then you can see the image. But if you change your viewpoint, the painting can simply look like a confusing mess of colors and lines. Some of the best examples of this kind of art can be seen on our city streets.

Julian Beever: Pavement king

The British artist Julian Beever is a special kind of pavement painter. For the last ten years, he has traveled all over Europe, creating chalk drawings that are also illusions. Beever's amazing illusions include a bathing beauty in a swimming pool, a seal surrounded by blocks of ice, and a giant fly.

Many of Beever's images play tricks on the public. One painting shows a pile of sand beside a deep hole in which some glistening treasures are revealed. People approaching the work do a "double-take" as they see the treasures below their feet. Another Beever painting shows a gaping hole in the pavement, with a large paving slab moved to one side. As people approach this painting, they swerve to one side to avoid the hole in the pavement. But when they look back, the illusion disappears! (You can find a website containing images of Beever's work on page 55.)

Kurt Wenner: Master street painter

Another leading street artist is the U.S. painter Kurt Wenner. He works mainly in Italy, where he creates spectacular works in front of large audiences. He is especially interested in creating an illusion of depth in his pavement paintings.

One of Wenner's most famous works is *Reflections*, which shows the reflections of two young couples in a pond. Wenner has also created several paintings showing desperate people trapped inside a pit. In these paintings, the artist uses his skills in perspective and foreshortening to create the illusion that a large hole has opened up in the pavement.

The making of a master

Kurt Wenner studied at art school and then worked as a draftsman, making technical drawings for NASA (the National Aeronautics and Space Administration). In 1982 he moved to Italy, where he spent his time copying the paintings of the great masters, such as Michelangelo. One day Wenner was talking with a street artist, who asked if Wenner would like to paint the head of an angel while he was at lunch. This was the start of Wenner's career as a street artist! Now, Wenner paints at festivals and creates murals for people's homes

Wenner's work *Reflections* is partly a painting and partly performance art. The painting shows four figures reflected in a pool, while four actors take their place on the edge of the painting to complete the work.

Amazing anamoprhs

The pavement images described on pages 30 and 31 are all examples of **anamorphic art**. Anamorphs are images that have been specially created to be seen from a particular point of view. Some anamorphs can only be seen from a single viewpoint. Others make sense from several different angles, but they look much better when you approach them from the "correct" viewpoint.

Hidden anamorphs

Some artists have enjoyed creating hidden images that only a few people can read. One very famous anamorph can be found in a painting by the 16th-century artist Hans Holbein. The painting is called *The Ambassadors*.

Holbein's *The Ambassadors* shows two rich and intelligent young men in a study. The portrait is very skillfully painted, but on the floor is a strange, gray-colored blur. In fact, this gray shape is a **distorted** image of a skull. If the shape is viewed from a particular point on the right of the painting, the distortion is corrected and you can clearly see that it is a skull, rather than a blur. Nobody knows exactly why Holbein chose to include a hidden image of a skull in his portrait. Perhaps it was intended to send out a message that even wealthy and intelligent people have to die.

Hans Holbein's *The Ambassadors* contains an anamorph of a skull, lying at the feet of the two young men. Try putting your face close to the page, slightly to the right of the picture. Then, close your left eye. You should be able to see the secret image of the skull.

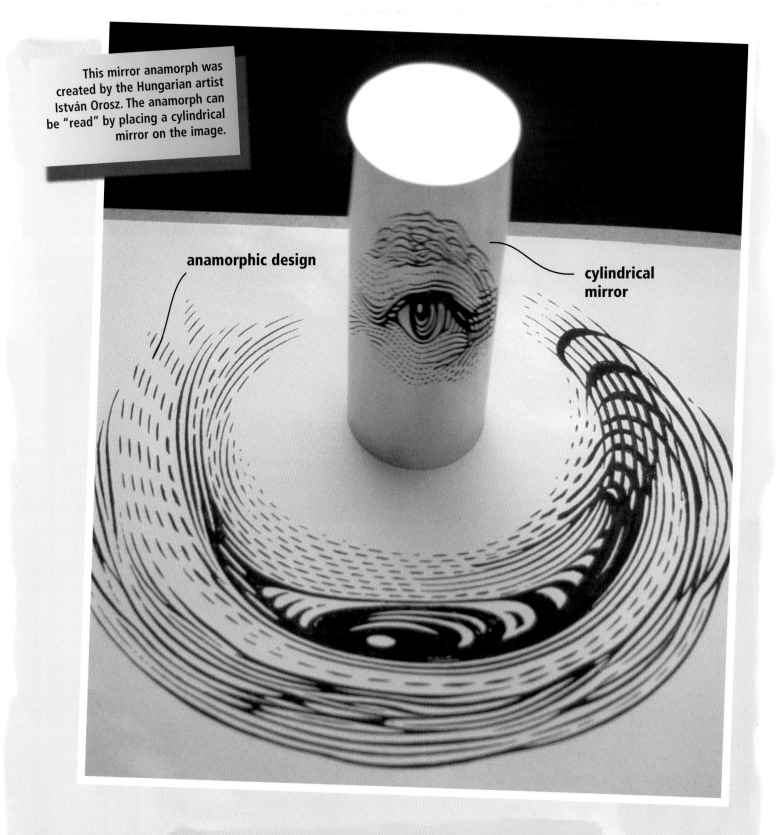

anamorphic design

cylindrical mirror

Look in the mirror!

Some anamorphs can only be read with the help of a mirror shaped like a cylinder. At first sight, most of these images simply appear to be wild, swirling patterns. However, when a cylindrical mirror is placed on the image, the secret meaning of the anamorph is revealed.

When a mirror anamorph is viewed as a reflection, the deliberate distortion in the image is corrected and a clear picture emerges. Mirror anamorphs were especially popular in 18th-century Holland. In the 19th century, publishers produced whole books of "magic mirror" images that were designed to be viewed with the help of a cylindrical mirror.

The secret in the mirror

How do artists create their mirror anamorphs? The answer is they need a cylindrical mirror—and a lot of practice! The artists look in the mirror as they make their drawings. They make sure they produce an image that looks exactly correct when it is reflected in the mirror. Once the mirror is removed, the anamorph cannot be seen. It can only be "read" by using a mirror that is exactly the same as the one the artist has used.

Kelly Houle

The U.S. artist Kelly Houle creates acrylic paintings that are also anamorphs. Houle's painting *The Veiled Woman* appears to show the petals of a flower, but when a cylindrical mirror is placed in the center of the "flower," the heads of three veiled women are revealed. Another painting, *Lighthouse,* presents the swirling waves of a storm, while hidden inside the picture is a lighthouse.

Secret portraits

After the English King Charles I was executed in 1649, his supporters sent each other anamorphic portraits of the king. They could look at the portraits by squinting at them sideways, but nobody else realized what the pictures showed.

István Orosz

The Hungarian artist István Orosz is a master of anamorphic art. Many of his mirror anamorphs are so skillful that they make sense as pictures in their own right, even before you add a cylindrical mirror.

Orosz painted *The Mysterious Island* as the cover for a novel by Jules Verne. The picture appears to show the island, but when it is viewed with the help of a cylindrical mirror, the face of Jules Verne is revealed.

Orosz's painting *The Well* works in the same way. It shows a well inside a mysterious garden. However, the garden also contains the hidden face of the artist M. C. Escher.

István Orosz's *The Mysterious Island* shows explorers in a wild landscape. But it also contains an anamorphic portrait: the bearded face of the author Jules Verne.

Changing images

Sometimes artists create images that can be "read" in more than one way. These pictures are known as **metamorphs**, a name that comes from the ancient Greek word for "changing shape." Some metamorphs are quite simple to create, but others are sophisticated works of art.

Dali's disappearing images

The 20th-century Spanish artist Salvador Dali was fascinated by the shifting images of dreams. He painted several dreamlike paintings that work as metamorphs, gradually changing from one image into another.

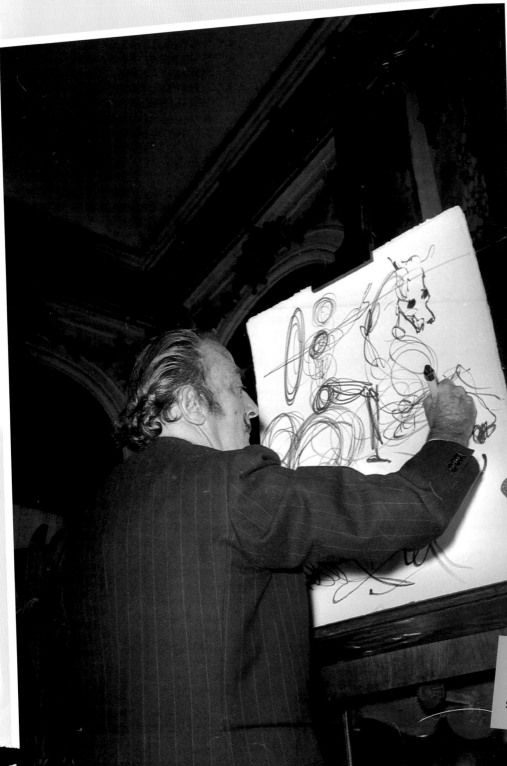

Dali painted a series of portraits that can also be viewed as scenes. His most famous changing portrait has the title *The Image Disappears*. At first sight, the painting seems to be a portrait of a bearded man, but after you have looked at it for a while, this image disappears and another picture takes its place. The second picture shows a young girl reading a letter in a room draped by a curtain.

In 1939 Dali created a portrait for the cover of the French magazine *Match*. At first glance, it shows the face of a leading war general. But a closer look also reveals a battle scene. One of Dali's strangest metamorphs dates from 1976. This painting of his wife gazing out to sea becomes a portrait of Abraham Lincoln when it is viewed from farther away.

This photograph shows Spanish artist Salvador Dali at work in his studio. Dali enjoyed creating playful images that seem to change as you look at them.

Modern metamorphs

Two contemporary artists who create metamorphs are the Mexican painter Octavio Ocampo and the Swiss master of illusions Sandro Del Prete.

Ocampo specializes in portraits. *The General's Family* presents the figure of a bald, bearded man facing to one side. However, if you look carefully at this portrait, nine other faces emerge! Ocampo's painting *Forever Always* appears to show an old man and woman facing each other, but hidden in the painting is a picture of the couple when they were young.

Sandro Del Prete's *Saint George the Dragon Slayer* appears at first sight to be a simple portrait of the head of the saint set against a background of woods and castle. But when you look carefully at George's head, you can see the scene of Saint George mounted on his horse fighting the dragon. Interestingly, the head of Saint George on his horse also contains the picture of the fight.

Try it yourself

Try making your own metamorph. This simple metamorph shows a vase, but it is also a double portrait. Try changing the features of the two characters to alter the shape of the vase. Perhaps the double portrait could be two versions of you?

A metamorph to make yourself: Is it a vase or a double portrait?

Looking at metamorphs

Take a look at the portrait below. Do you think it shows a young girl or an old woman? Or is it hard to make up your mind? Looking at a metamorph like this can make you feel quite uncomfortable. This is because your brain cannot decide exactly what you are seeing.

A confusing portrait: What do you think it shows?

Human beings have an instinct to "make sense" of shapes and patterns, so when you look at a picture, your brain makes an instant decision about what the picture shows. Using the evidence provided by your eyes, your brain makes a "best guess" about the subject of the picture. Usually your brain gets it right, but this process is not so easy when you are looking at metamorphs. Your brain cannot decide which subject is the best guess, so the picture seems to flip between two choices.

The choice that your brain prefers depends on where you look in the picture. In the metamorph on this page, looking to the left of the picture provides strong evidence for the young woman. However, if you look at the girl's neck (the old woman's mouth), there is stronger evidence for the old woman, so that is what you see.

Upside-down images

Some images have been very cleverly designed so that they can be reversed. They can be seen "right way up" and "upside down" and still make sense either way.

In the 1890s U.S. comic book artist Peter Newell produced a set of simple images, known as "Topsy Turvys," that could be read right way up and upside down. Ten years later Dutch artist Gustave Verbeek created his "Upside Downs," which were detailed reversible scenes that each told a story.

Reversible portraits

The British artist Rex Whistler, who lived in the first half of the 20th century, created an amazing series of reversible portraits. These portraits were designed to show different faces, depending on which way up the image was viewed. *Young and Old Man* shows the same man in youth and in old age. *Sad and Happy* shows two men in very different moods. *Royals* is a reversible portrait of a king and a queen. (Look on page 55 for details of a website containing images of Whistler's work.)

Scottish artist John Kay's 18th-century portrait *The Lawyer or the Client?* can be read in two ways. It is either a smiling lawyer or, if you turn the book upside down, a scowling client.

THE CLIENT. K 1790

THE LAWYER. 1790

Try it yourself

Why not try creating your own reversible portrait that can be read the right way up and upside down? The portrait you produce will need to have a big chin (which could be a nose) and a big nose (which could be a chin). You will also have to be quite inventive about hats (or wigs). Look at the picture of the lawyer and client on this page to help you create your portrait.

Puzzling Patterns

Illusion art is not just about pictures. Artists can also create amazing visual effects by using pattern and color. Artists such as M. C. Escher use repeating patterns to create the illusion of constantly shifting shapes and points of view. But how do they do it?

Tessellating patterns

In the 1920s Escher began to experiment with making patterns from identical shapes that all fitted exactly together. This kind of effect is known as a **tessellating pattern**. Most traditional tessellating patterns are made from regular geometric shapes. Squares, diamonds, and hexagons can all be used. The one important rule to remember is that the shapes must be **symmetrical**.

Most tessellating patterns use a limited number of regular geometric shapes, but there is still plenty of room to experiment. Artists can combine regular shapes of different sizes. They can also combine different shapes, such as squares and hexagons.

Color is also very important. By using contrasting colors, it is possible to create some amazing optical illusions. Tessellating shapes can seem to come out of the page toward the viewer and then suddenly flip direction.

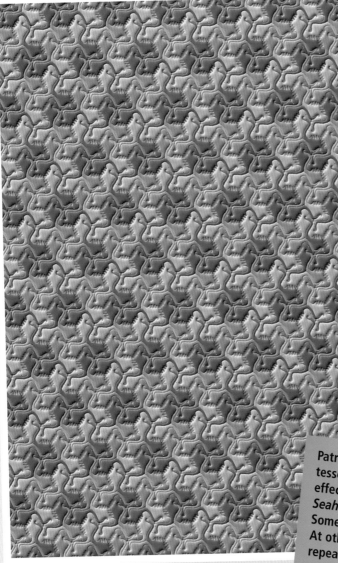

Patrick Snels is a Dutch artist who uses tessellating patterns to create unusual visual effects. As you look at this picture, called *Seahorses*, you keep seeing different things. Sometimes you notice individual seahorses. At other times you see a larger pattern of repeating blue hexagons.

Try it yourself

Why not try making a 3D tessellating pattern? This tessellating pattern is made from hexagons and diamonds. Once it is colored in, it is also an optical illusion.

1 First, draw a square that measures 3 inches by 3 inches (8 centimeters by 8 centimeters). Then, create a grid by drawing light pencil lines 0.25 inches (5 millimeters) apart (see Figure 1). If you have a photocopier, make lots of copies of your grid. You will need the same grid to create the pattern on page 43. The extra grids will also be very useful if you make a mistake, or if you want to create some tessellating patterns of your own.

2 On your grid, draw several rows of crosses, as in Figure 2. Remember to leave a gap between each row. When you have finished, you will see that you have created alternate rows of hexagon and diamond shapes.

3 In the empty rows draw a zigzag line—marked in red on Figure 3.

4 Mark the vertical lines shown in blue on Figure 3. Now you have drawn a series of cubes.

5 Color in the faces of the cubes, as in Figure 4, to create a 3D effect.

Now you have created an optical illusion made up of 3D cubes. Which way up are the cubes?

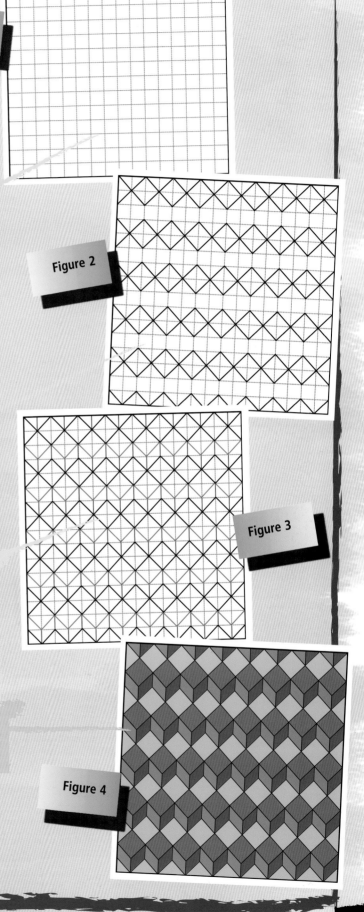

Figure 1

Figure 2

Figure 3

Figure 4

Surprising shapes

Escher transformed the art of tessellation. Instead of simply using geometric shapes, he created tessellating patterns from a huge range of surprising shapes. Altogether, Escher created hundreds of tessellating shapes in the form of fish, birds, dogs, crabs, insects, horses, humans, and other beasts.

Escher's shapes are not regular, so in order to tessellate they need to face in opposite directions. Some of his patterns show two flocks of birds (painted in contrasting colors) flying in opposite directions across the page. Others show shoals of fish. In his sequence of prints called *Sky and Water*, bird and fish shapes are combined.

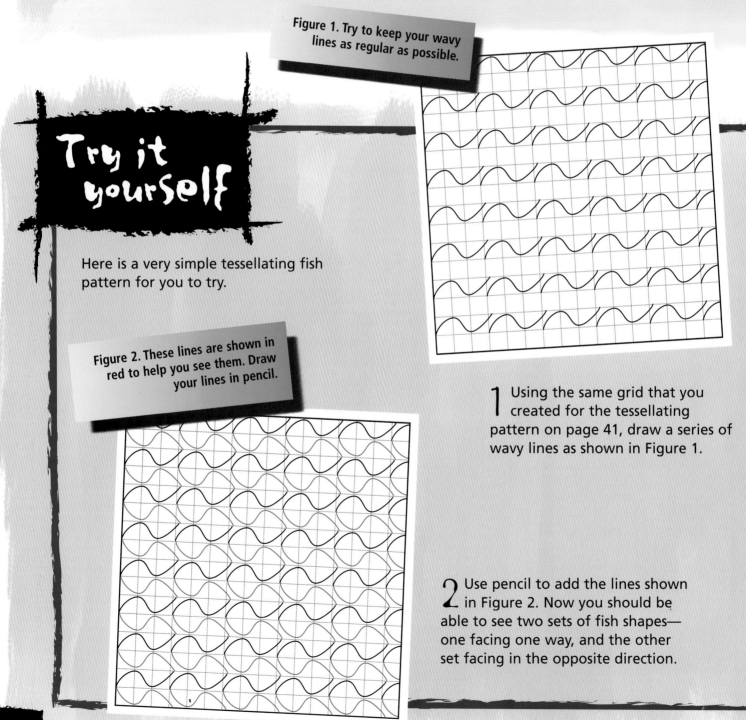

Figure 1. Try to keep your wavy lines as regular as possible.

Try it yourself

Here is a very simple tessellating fish pattern for you to try.

Figure 2. These lines are shown in red to help you see them. Draw your lines in pencil.

1 Using the same grid that you created for the tessellating pattern on page 41, draw a series of wavy lines as shown in Figure 1.

2 Use pencil to add the lines shown in Figure 2. Now you should be able to see two sets of fish shapes—one facing one way, and the other set facing in the opposite direction.

Since Escher's time, many other artists have created tessellating patterns using unusual shapes. Today's artists often use computer programs to help them create their patterns. Look on page 55 for details of a website that gives instructions on how to make your own computer tessellations. You will also find fascinating information on the mathematics of tessellation.

When you look at a tessellating pattern, your brain is constantly flipping from one interpretation to another. Sometimes you see the whole design and sometimes you see the detail. You will also find your brain flipping between the different shapes. So, in a pattern made up of birds and fish, sometimes it is only possible to see the birds and sometimes you only see the fish.

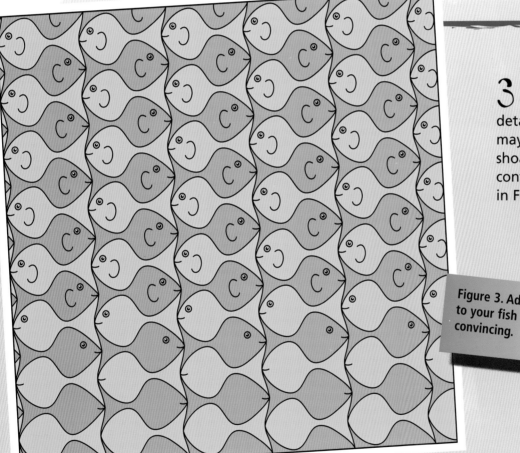

3 Add eyes, gills, tail fins, and any other details to your fish. You may like to show the two shoals of fish in two contrasting colors, as in Figure 3.

Figure 3. Add color and details to your fish to make them look convincing.

Now that you have created this simple tessellation, why not try creating some patterns of your own. How about a pattern of birds and fish?

43

Optical Investigations

Some artists use their knowledge of how our eyes work to experiment with **optical** effects. Their paintings use color, shapes, and pattern to play visual tricks on their viewers' eyes and brains.

Op Art

In the 1960s a group of artists became very interested in how we see. They used their knowledge to create experimental works of art. The art movement became known as **Op Art**, which is short for "optical art." Two of its leading members were Victor Vasarely and Bridget Riley.

Bridget Riley

The British painter Bridget Riley has been exploring the optical effects of colors and patterns for over 40 years. Many of her paintings use stripes or wavy lines to create some very disturbing visual effects. These paintings seem to shimmer and dance in front of your eyes.

In her painting *Sheng-Tung*, Bridget Riley experiments with line and color to create a powerful optical effect. How many colors can you see in this painting?

Victor Vasarely

The Hungarian artist Vasarely is known as the "father of Op Art." His paintings use mainly geometric shapes, such as squares and triangles. In his paintings, Vasarely puts strongly contrasting colors (such as black and white) next to each other to create a vibrating effect. He often also deliberately distorts his shapes so that parts of his painting seem to bulge toward the viewer. (Look on page 55 for details of a website containing images of Vasarely's work.)

A confusing optical illusion: Are the green lines parallel or bent?

Op Art takes off!

Op Art became very popular in the 1960s and 1970s, when the patterns created by artists like Riley were used for posters and advertisements. Fashion designers created Op Art clothes with stripes, swirls, and dots, in strongly contrasting colors or black and white.

Can you believe your eyes?

Take a look at the picture above. Do you think the gray lines are parallel? In fact they are. This image demonstrates how color and pattern can create some very confusing optical effects. If you continue to stare at the image, you may notice some other strange effects. Some of the strips may appear to bulge toward you. You may also start to see some 3D stairs.

45

Curious colors

Do you think you can trust the way you see colors? Try the "Changing colors test" below and think again! Several U.S. artists have explored the strange visual effects that can be produced when you put certain colors together.

Artist Richard Anuszkiewicz puts very bright colors side by side. As you look at his paintings, the colors seem to "fight" each other.

This results in a luminous effect that can sometimes even be seen as flashes of light.

Artist Kenneth Noland creates "target" paintings whose color rings seem to widen and narrow as you look at them. Artist Larry Poons has produced several brightly colored canvases scattered with small colored dots. As you look at these paintings, the dots start to dance around in front of your eyes.

Changing colors test

Look carefully at this picture. How many colors can you see (apart from white)? Most people will answer four, but the real answer is two. The color that you see depends on what other colors are surrounding it.

How many colors do you see here?

Painting with dots

As early as the 1880s, a group of French artists tried an interesting experiment with color. Instead of mixing colors on their palettes and then painting a picture, they created paintings in which the viewer's eyes did the job of mixing the colors.

The artists painted their pictures from thousands of tiny colored dots. These dots were all shades of primary colors—red, yellow, and blue—and were grouped together in different combinations to make up the colors the artists wanted to show.

When the viewer looked at the pictures from a distance, all the dots combined to make up the different colors. The effect of these paintings was light and sparkling, but it was very hard to create a sense of depth.

Painting with dots is called pointillism ("point" is French for "dot"). The leading member of the pointillist movement was Georges Seurat. He created a series of landscape paintings using the pointillist technique. Two of his most famous paintings show people relaxing by a riverbank in Paris. Each of these paintings took several years to complete.

In his pointillist painting *Bathers at Asnières*, Georges Seurat tried to recreate the experience of seeing a sparkling, light-filled scene.

Taking It further

Do you think you would enjoy a career as an illusion artist? Perhaps you would like to work as a designer, visualizing your projects in 3D? Or maybe you would like to produce super-realist fantasy art for video games and movies?

Are you interested in finding out more about the way our brains work when we see shapes, patterns, and colors? Or maybe you are fascinated by the mathematical ideas that lie behind illusion art? Whatever your interest in illusion art, there are many ways to take the subject further.

3D and illusion art as a career

Many different careers require the skill of thinking in 3D. Architects, draftsmen, and interior designers all need to show their ideas in 3D. Car and plane designers use the rules of perspective to create their computer models. Set designers for movies and the theater create their 3D illusions using sketches, computer designs, and miniature models.

An industrial designer uses a computer to help him create a model vehicle. This photograph was taken at the Renault Technocenter Workshops.

Comic and fantasy artists use the skills of illusion art to create their imaginary worlds. Fashion and textile designers experiment with shapes, colors, and patterns to create new eye-catching designs.

Some artists devote their careers to exploring the possibilities of illusion art. Who knows—maybe you may be the next Escher, taking art in directions that no one has ever imagined before!

What next?

Whatever career you decide to follow, you will first need to be trained. Most designers and artists start by going to art college, where they can study many different areas, ranging from Fine Art to Product Design. You can use the Internet or your local library to find out more about the amazing range of art and design classes available.

Career profile: Industrial designer

Ben Taylor is an industrial designer who has always been interested in illusion art. At college he studied industrial design and 3D and learned how to create computer models of vehicles and machines. In the early years of his career, Ben worked as a draftsman for a sports equipment firm and a toy manufacturer. Now he is a freelance designer, creating designs for **prototype** cars for several major motor companies. Ben works almost entirely on computer, using **CAD** (computer-aided design) programs. Even though his work has a practical application, he uses the skills of illusion art every day. The super-realistic images he creates appear to be solid and 3D.

49

Building a portfolio

If you apply to an art college, you will need to show a **portfolio** of your work and ideas. It is never too early to get started on this. Keep all the notes and sketches you make. It is amazing how fast they pile up!

Why not get into the habit of keeping a sketchbook, so that you can make rapid drawings or jot down ideas when they occur to you? Add notes to your sketches saying what you are trying to achieve and suggesting some possible new directions you could take.

Keeping notes and sketches will remind you about your ideas and help you to explain your art to other people. It is also very rewarding to look back at your sketchbook and see how much progress you have made.

Start to collect postcards or photocopies of artists' work that you admire. If you are thinking of becoming a designer, you could cut out pictures from magazines or take photographs of designs that appeal to you. All these images will give you inspiration, and you can return to them whenever you need new ideas.

A portfolio is an important record of all the ideas that you have been exploring.

Studying perception

Perhaps this book has made you wonder about the way your eyes and brain work when you see images. The science of perception is a fascinating area of study. There are some suggestions for websites to look at and books to read on pages 54 and 55. Scientists who study perception usually begin with a science or medical major, but you can also major in neuroscience, the study of the brain and nerves.

Mathematical ideas

Maybe you enjoy math? If so, you can discover more about the mathematics of perspective and tessellation by following the website link on page 55. Some mathematicians devote their careers to studying these fascinating topics.

Look again!

Looking at illusion art is fun. It can make you think really hard, and it can make you realize that things are not always what they seem!

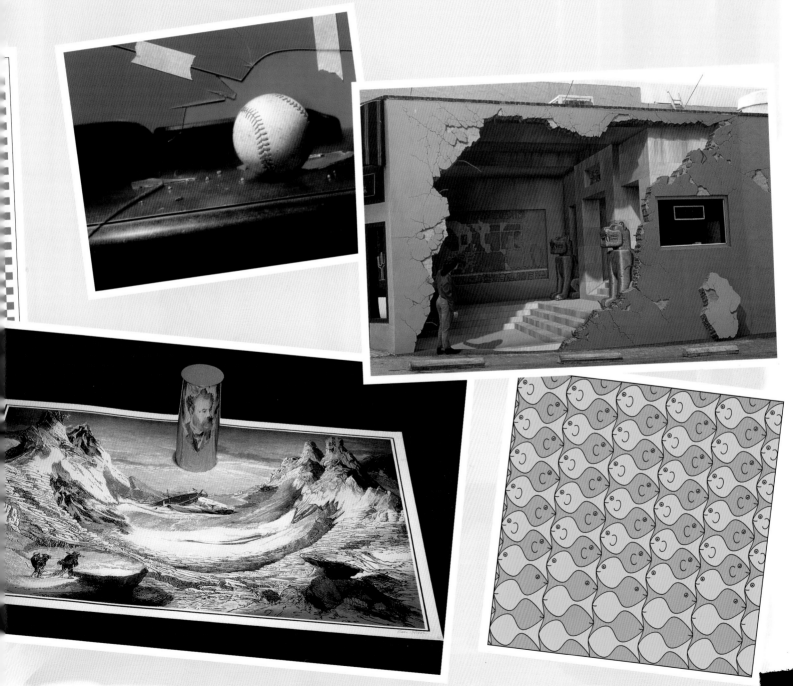

Glossary

2D having two dimensions: width and height. When something is 2D, it has no depth and looks flat.

3D having three dimensions: width, height, and depth. 3D is short for "three dimensional." When something is painted so it looks 3D, it looks solid, not flat.

acrylic non-oily paint that is made from chemicals

airbrush brush that uses compressed air to blow paint onto a surface

anamorphic art art that is specially created to be seen from a particular point of view

animations series of drawings that are filmed very quickly, one after the other, so that the objects in the drawings appear to move

atmospheric perspective visual effect in which things in the distance seem to grow paler and become less clear

backdrop large painted screen or curtain hanging at the back of a stage

CAD type of computer software that allows designers to create images in 3D. "CAD" is short for "computer-aided design."

cartoon full-sized sketch of a painting, from which the final work is traced or copied

construction lines lines drawn by artists to help them show objects and people in perspective

distort to change something so that it loses its usual shape

engineering science of designing machines and structures such as bridges

fantasy something created by the imagination

flats tall, painted boards that are placed at an angle on either side of a stage

foreground front part of a picture or a scene. Foreground is the opposite of background.

foreshortening technique used by artists to show objects coming straight toward the viewer

futuristic about things that might happen in the future

grid network of horizontal and vertical lines, used as a guide

highlight area of lighter tone in a painting or drawing

horizon line line marking the place where the sky and the land (or sea) seem to meet

horizontal parallel to the ground

interior inside space, such as a room

metamorph image that can be read in more than one way

mural wall painting

one-point perspective system of drawing in perspective, using a single vanishing point

Op Art art movement that began in the 1960s, in which the artists experimented with optical effects. "Op Art" is short for "optical art."

optical to do with eyesight and seeing

optical illusion something that you think you see, but that is not really there

perspective technique used by artists to show the relationship between close and distant objects

perspective box box with a small eyehole through which a picture (or a series of pictures) can be viewed

photorealism style of painting that is so realistic that a painting looks like a photograph

portfolio collection of drawings, photographs, and more that displays the work and interests of an artist or a designer

prototype first version of an invention, used for experiment and development

shading darker areas of a drawing or painting. Shading helps give the impression that an object is solid.

super-realism style of painting that is so realistic the painting looks like a photograph

symmetrical perfectly balanced, with both sides exactly the same

tessellating pattern pattern made from identical shapes that all fit together

texture feel of something, especially its roughness or smoothness

three-point perspective system of drawing in perspective, using three vanishing points

trompe l'oeil style used by artists to trick viewers into believing that what they see is real

two-point perspective system of drawing in perspective, using two vanishing points

vanishing point point on the horizon of a painting where all the parallel lines in the painting appear to meet

vertical upright, or at right angles to the ground

visual effect way that something looks to the viewer

Find Out More

More books to read

Gooding, Mel, and Julian Rothenstein (eds.). *The Playful Eye*. San Francisco: Chronicle, 2000.

Gregory, Richard L. *Eye and Brain: The Psychology of Seeing*. Princeton, N.J.: Princeton University Press, 1997.

Locker, J. L. *The Magic of M. C. Escher*. New York: Harry N. Abrams, 2000.

Schattscheider, Doris. *M. C. Escher: Visions of Symmetry*. New York: Harry N. Abrams, 2nd ed., 2004.

Seckel, Al. *The Great Book of Optical Illusions*. Buffalo, N.Y.: Firefly, repr. ed., 2005.

Seckel, Al. *Masters of Deception: Escher, Dali & the Artists of Optical Illusion*. New York: Sterling, 2004.

Useful websites

The art of M. C. Escher, "impossible perspectives," and other visual tricks

http://www.mcescher.com
http://www.etropolis.com/escher
Good examples of Escher's art.

http://members.lycos.nl/amazingart
Examples of "impossible images" and more.

http://www.planetperplex.com/en/impossible_perspective/html
http://www.planetperplex.com/en/rob_gonsalves.html
Examples of "impossible perspective" and Rob Gonsalves's perspective puzzle paintings (see pages 18–19).

http://www.patrickhughes.co.uk
Patrick Hughes's "reverspectives" (see page 18).

Trompe l'oeil and super-realism

http://www.artlex.com
An art dictionary. Click on "Tr–Tz" to find examples of *trompe l'oeil* art, including several Dutch and U.S. letter-rack paintings (see page 22). Click on "Pf–Pim" to find examples of photorealist art (see page 25).

http://www.thewaichulisstudio.net
Some modern *trompe l'oeil* paintings (see page 24).

http://www.ralphlgoings.com
Ralph Goings's photorealist paintings (see page 25).

http://www.designboom.com/eng/funclub/duanehanson.html
Duane Hanson's super-realistic sculpted figures (see page 26).

http://www.scrubbles.net/sydmead.html
Examples of Syd Mead's fantasy art (see page 26).

Street paintings

http://www.illusion-art.com/default.asp
John Pugh's website (see pages 4–5, 28–29).

http://users.skynet.be/J.Beever/index.html
Julian Beever's website (see page 30).

http://www.kurtwenner.com
Kurt Wenner's website (see pages 30–31).

Anamorphs and metamorphs

http://www.anamorphosis.com
Great examples of anamorphs. Includes
instructions to download free software to create
your own anamorphs.

http://www.planetperplex.com/en/istvan_
orosz.html
http://www.planetperplex.com/en/
upsidedown.html
Examples of anamorphs by István Orosz (see
pages 34–35) and upside-down images by Peter
Newell, Gustave Verbeek, and Rex Whistler (see
pages 38–39).

http://www.ambigram.com/matchbox/
Reversible images on vintage matchboxes.

Tessellating patterns

http://library.thinkquest.org/16661/
A website devoted to the art and science of
tessellation. Includes mathematical
explanations of tessellation and downloadable
templates for creating tessellations.

Op Art and optical experiments

http://www.artnet.com
For examples of Victor Vasarely's art (see pages
44–45), type "Victor Vasarely" in the search box.

http://www.mishabittleston.com/artists/
bridget_riley/
Bridget Riley's works and interviews (see pages
44–45).

http://www.sharecom.ca/noland/
The works of Kenneth Noland (see page 46).

Depth and distance

http://www2.evansville.edu/studiochalkboard
Click "enter." Perspective and atmospheric
perspective are explained. Includes exercises in
using perspective.

2D (two-dimensional space) 5, 20
3D (three-dimensional space) 5, 6, 9, 12, 13, 20, 26, 41, 45, 48

airbrush technique 27
anamorphic art 32–35
animations 26
Anuszkiewicz, Richard 46
atmospheric perspective 8

Beever, Julian 30
Bell, Charles 25
Brega, David 24
Brunelleschi, Philippo 7
Brunelli, Anthony 11
Burgh, Hendrik van der 12

CAD (computer-aided design) 49
careers in art 48–49
cartoons 29
Claude Lorraine 8
Close, Chuck 25
color 6, 8, 27, 40, 44, 45, 46, 47
Colyer, Edwaert 23
comic strip art 14
construction lines 7, 9, 10, 11
Cottingham, Robert 25

Dali, Salvador 36
Del Prete, Sandro 37
depth and distance 6–15, 30

Escher, M. C. 16–17, 20, 21, 35, 40, 42
Estes, Richard 25

fantasy art 26, 49
foreshortening 6, 14–15, 26, 30

Goings, Ralph 25
Gonsalves, Rob 18

Hanson, Duane 26
Harnett, William 22
Holbein, Hans 32
Hooch, Pieter de 12

horizon line 7, 9, 10
Houle, Kelly 34
Hughes, Patrick 18

"impossible" images 5, 16, 20
industrial design 48, 49
interiors 12

Kay, John 39

letter-rack painting 22–23, 24
Levine, Marilyn 26
light 8, 29, 46, 47
    highlights and reflections 25, 27

mathematics 48, 51
Mead, Syd 26–27
metamorphs 36–38
Michelangelo 15, 30
mirror anamorphs 33–35
murals 4, 28–29, 30

Newell, Peter 38
Noland, Kenneth 46

Ocampo, Octavio 37
Op Art 44–45
optical illusions 4, 5, 18, 19, 20, 30, 44–46
Orosz, István 33, 34–35

patterns 40–43, 44, 45
pavement art 30–31, 32
perception, science of 51
performance art 31
perspective 6–15, 26, 30, 48
    atmospheric perspective 8
    one-, two-, and three-point perspective 10–11
    reverspectives 18
    trick perspective 16–20
perspective boxes 12
Peto, John Frederick 22
photorealism 22, 25
    see also super-realism
pointillism 47

Poons, Larry 46
portfolio, building a 50
Pugh, John 4, 28–29

Rembrandt 22
reversible images 38–39
reverspectives 18
Riley, Bridget 44, 45

sculpture 26
Seurat, Georges 47
sfumato 8
shading and shadows 6, 8, 9, 16, 24, 26, 27, 29
shapes, changing 20
Snels, Patrick 40
Springfield, Molly 24
stage set design 13, 48
super-realism 22–29, 49
    fantasy art 26, 49
    photorealism 25
    sculpture 26
    trompe l'oeil 22–24, 28–29

tessellation 40–43
toy theaters 13
trompe l'oeil 22–24, 28–29

upside-down images 38–39

vanishing point 7, 9, 10, 11, 16
Vasarely, Victor 44, 45
Verbeek, Gustave 38
Vermeer, Jan 12
viewpoints 30–39
    anamorphic art 32–35
    metamorphs 36–38
    pavement art 30–31, 32
    reversible images 38–39
    trick perspective 16–20
visuals 26

Waichulis, Anthony 5, 24
Wenner, Kurt 6, 30–31
Whistler, Rex 39
Wright, Stuart Pearson 13